Make it with

Papier-mâché

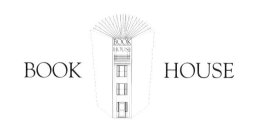

BOOK HOUSE

© Copyright for the English edition for the UK
and British Commonwealth by Book House

Original title: ¡Vamos a Crear! Papel maché
© Parramon Ediciones, S.A., 2002

Published in Great Britain in 2003 by
Book House, an imprint of
The Salariya Book Company Ltd
25 Marlborough Place, Brighton BN1 1UB

Visit the Salariya Book Company at
www.salariya.com
www.book-house.co.uk

ISBN 1 904194 99 0

A catalogue record for this book is available from the British Library.

Printed and bound in Spain.

Contents

Contents Contents Contents

Introduction

Introduction

Introduction

Papier-mâché is nothing more than torn paper mixed with glue. *Mâché* comes from the French word 'mâcher' (mah-shay), which means to tear apart or to chew. In the English language, papier-mâché refers to torn, glued paper that is moulded into shapes.

You can make papier-mâché from almost any type of paper, including newspaper, magazine pages and tissue paper. However, it is newspaper that is usually used. Thin cardboard can be used too. You can also buy instant papier-mâché mix, which is a paper powder you mix with water. The instant mixture is very easy to model.

This book shows you different ways to work with papier-mâché, using clay moulds, plastic moulds, cardboard tubes, egg boxes, balloons and many other materials. The twelve colourful projects also show you how to apply different finishes, including paint, tissue paper and even aluminium foil. You can turn a plain plastic bowl into an artistic object, an egg box into a turtle and even a cardboard toilet tissue tube can become a space rocket!

Most of the tools you will need to make these projects are things you use every day, either at school or at home. They include scissors, glue, paints, clay, sticky tape, string, pieces of wire and just about any kind of paper.

The projects in this book use water-soluble powdered glue or white glue diluted with water to make the papier-mâché. Either type of glue can be used for any of the projects.

Some projects tell you to soak the paper in water, while others do not. Wet paper is not always necessary, but for certain projects, wet paper is easier to shape and gives your finished piece more detail. Several projects also tell you to cover the dried papier-mâché with plaster paste. To make the paste, use plaster of paris, which is a chalky white powder. You may have used plaster of paris for other kinds of art or craft projects. Mix plaster of paris powder with water until it is about as thick as paint. Remember that plaster paste hardens quickly, especially if it is too thick.

Watch for special instructions at the end of each project to try other great ideas. Sometimes making just one small change creates a very different result.

REMEMBER!
Whenever you see this symbol, or when you are using scissors, ask an adult to help you.

Friendly Ghost
Friendly Ghost
Friendly Ghost

Friendly Ghost

Most people just use a white sheet to make a ghost. You can be more creative!

1 Form the shape of a bell with a big lump of modelling clay.

2 Mix powdered glue with water, then tear sheets of paper into small pieces. Soak the pieces of paper in the glue. Cover the clay bell with the glue-soaked paper.

Toolbox

You will need:
• modelling clay
• powdered glue
• paper
• scissors
• plaster of paris
• blue, black and white paints

3 When the paper is dry remove the clay. Use scissors to cut around the bottom of the paper figure to even out the edge.

6

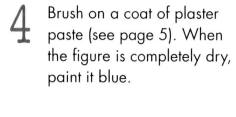

4   Brush on a coat of plaster paste (see page 5). When the figure is completely dry, paint it blue.

This little ghost is easy to make – and it will not scare your friends away!

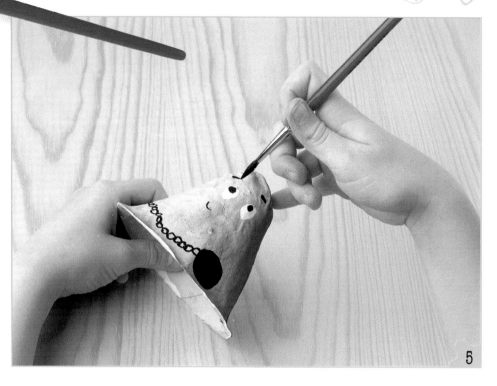

5

5   When the blue paint is dry, use black and white paints to add eyes, eyebrows, a mouth and a ball and chain.

Let your imagination soar

Other ideas:
Make lots of ghosts! If you paint them all different colours and give them all different expressions, you will have a ghostly family.

Bright Bird

When you make this exotic bird, give it brightly-coloured tissue-paper feathers – the brighter, the better!

Toolbox

You will need:
- scissors
- thin, flexible wire
- masking tape
- newspaper
- powdered glue
- paper
- paintbrush
- green, orange and yellow tissue paper
- orange, red and white modelling clay

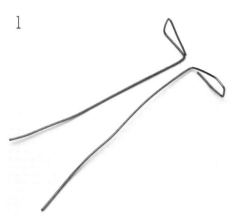

1 Cut two pieces of wire. Make each piece 15 cm long. Bend one end of each piece of wire into the shape of a triangle. The triangles will form the bird's feet.

2 Use masking tape to attach the straight end of each piece of wire to the two lower corners of a page of newspaper.

3 Crumple the newspaper to shape the body and the head of the bird. Wrap masking tape around the newspaper to hold the shape.

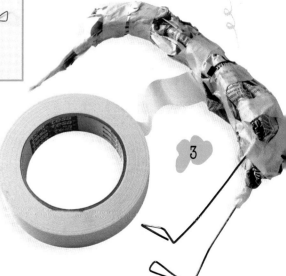

4 Mix powdered glue with water. Soak torn pieces of paper in the glue. Cover the body, head, beak and wire feet with glue-soaked paper. Cut shapes out of paper that look like wings and a tail and attach them to the bird's body.

5 When the paper is completely dry, brush glue all over it and attach torn pieces of green, orange and yellow tissue paper.

Let your imagination decide what shape your bird will be. Then imagine other animals and make them too!

6 To make the bird's eyes, roll small pieces of orange, red and white modelling clay into little balls. Stack the balls one on top of another – first orange, then red, then white. Using your fingers, press each eye onto the bird's head.

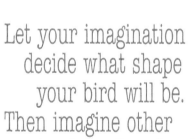

Let your imagination soar

Other ideas:
Glue the feet to a cardboard or wooden platform so your bird can stand by itself.

9

Hot-air Balloon

Use a party balloon to make this papier-mâché creation and let your imagination soar!

1. Blow up a balloon and knot it to hold in the air. Mix powdered glue with water, then tear coloured paper into strips. Coat the paper strips with glue and cover the balloon with them, leaving some space uncovered at the bottom.

Toolbox

You will need:
- balloon
- powdered glue
- purple, green and pink coloured paper
- paintbrushes
- bradawl
- red string
- paper
- glass
- orange and red paints
- scissors
- clear sticky tape

2. When the paper is dry use a bradawl to pop the balloon and to make a hole at the top of the paper balloon. Thread a loop of red string through the hole and knot the ends inside the balloon.

3. Tear paper into strips and soak the strips in glue. Press these strips into a glass to cover the inside of the glass.

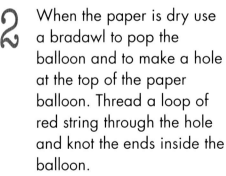
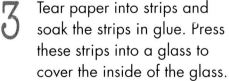

4 When the paper is dry take it out of the glass. This shape is the balloon's basket. Paint the basket orange with red stripes.

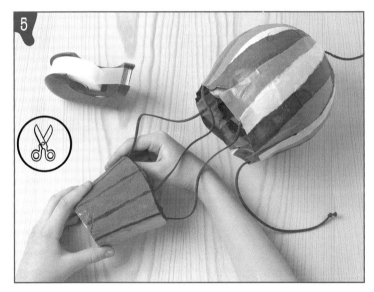

5 Cut four pieces of red string, each piece 20 cm long. Stick one end of each piece of string to the balloon with sticky tape and then stick the other end to the basket. Leave the same amount of space between each string.

Hang your balloon from the ceiling and prepare for an adventure. Think of the places you could go in this unusual form of transport!

Let your imagination soar

Other ideas:
Cover the balloon's basket with string or wool. Add other details, such as sandbags, made of tissue paper hanging from string.

11

Handsome Hanger

Your clothes deserve good-looking hangers. Decorating hangers is easy and a lot of fun – try it yourself.

1 Mix powdered glue with water. Cover a wooden coat hanger with several layers of newspaper strips that have been brushed with glue.

2 Cover the newspaper with glue-coated strips of yellow wrapping paper.

Toolbox

You will need:
- powdered glue
- newspaper
- paintbrush
- wooden coat hanger
- yellow wrapping paper
- white and purple paper
- black felt-tip pen
- scissors

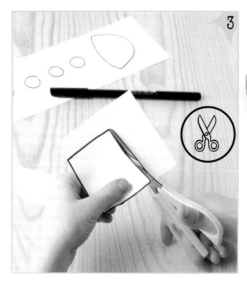

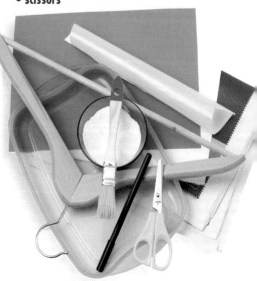

3 On a piece of white paper draw a pocket, a neck piece and four buttons and cut out the drawings.

12

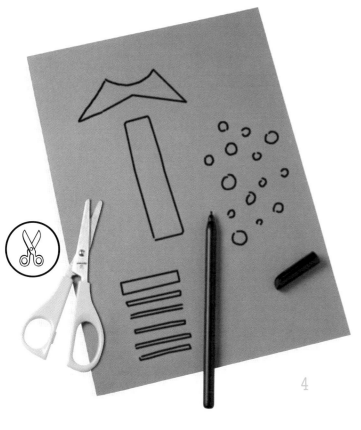

4 On a sheet of purple paper draw a collar, a long strip for the buttons, some stripes for the pocket and a lot of spots. Cut out all the drawings.

5 Glue the white and purple pieces onto the yellow wrapping paper to make one side of the hanger look like a shirt. Brush a coat of glue over the decorated surface.

A decorated hanger
can add colour to your
cloakroom and do
wonders for
your wardrobe!

Let your imagination soar

Other ideas:
Add a paper tie
or a bow to dress
up your hanger.

13

Little Red Devil

Little Red Devil
Little Red Devil
Little Red Devil

Toolbox

From head to trident, this bright red hand puppet is devilishly delightful and sinfully easy to make.

You will need:
- newspaper
- masking tape
- orange cardboard
- white glue
- paintbrushes
- instant papier-mâché
- plaster of paris
- red, white and black paints
- red felt
- felt-tip pen
- scissors
- needle
- black thread
- glue stick
- aluminium foil
- clear glue

1 Crumple newspaper into a ball and stick with masking tape. Roll a small piece of cardboard into a tube that fits around your middle finger and tape the tube closed. Tape the ball to the tube.

2 Dilute white glue with water. Wrap strips of glue-soaked newspaper around the newspaper ball and the cardboard tube.

3 Use instant papier-mâché to shape horns and a nose on the puppet's head and brush plaster paste (see page 5) over the whole head.

4 When the head is completely dry paint it red, then use white and black paints to make eyes and a mouth.

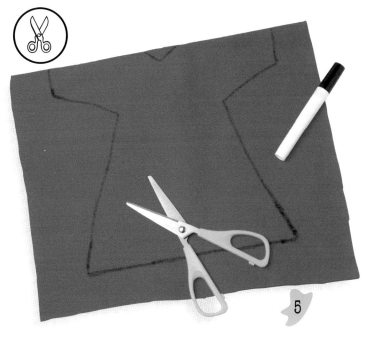

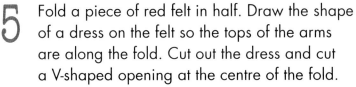

5 Fold a piece of red felt in half. Draw the shape of a dress on the felt so the tops of the arms are along the fold. Cut out the dress and cut a V-shaped opening at the centre of the fold.

6 Use a needle and black thread to sew the sides of the dress and under the arms. Do not sew across the bottom of the dress. Leave the neck and armholes open too.

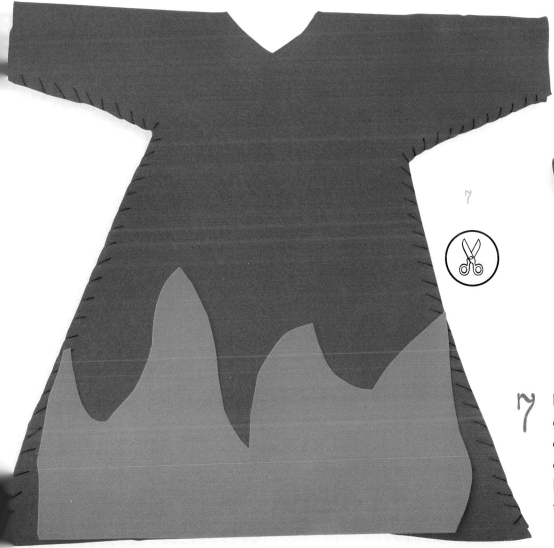

7 Draw the shape of flames on orange cardboard and cut it out. Use a glue stick to attach the flames along the bottom edge of the front of the dress.

15

8 Shape instant papier-mâché around your finger to make the puppet's two hands.

9 When the hands are dry paint them red.

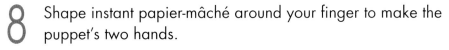

10 Make long, thin rolls of newspaper into the shape of a trident. Wrap masking tape around the newspaper to hold the shape.

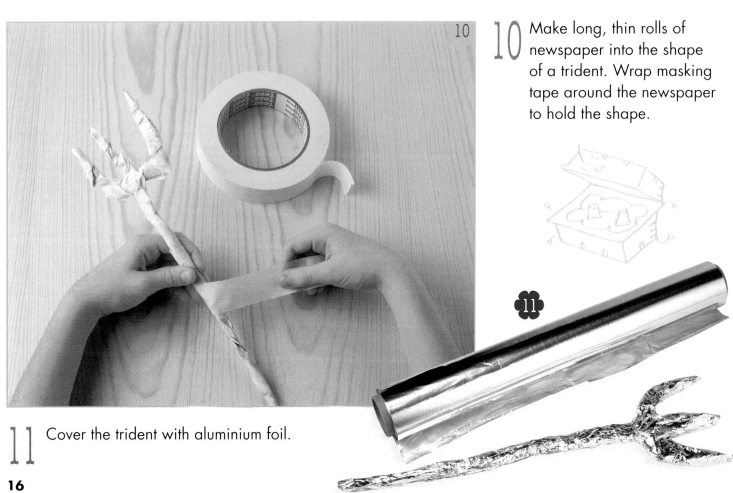

11 Cover the trident with aluminium foil.

12 To make a holder for the trident, cut two slits into the front of the dress, above the flames (as shown). Slide the handle of the trident into the top slit and out through the bottom slit. Finish the puppet by attaching its head and hands to the red felt dress with clear glue.

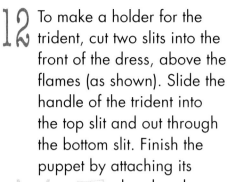

Now all you have to do is create a story.
    Your little red devil is ready to play the leading role.

Let your imagination soar

Other ideas:
Design a different dress, using materials such as plastic and crepe paper, to create a very different puppet character.

Designer Bowl Designer Bowl Designer Bowl Designer Bowl

Designer Bowl

Use a plastic bowl as a mould to make a fancy papier-mâché bowl. Decorate it any way you like – you're the designer!

1 Dilute white glue with water then tear newspaper into strips. Line the inside of a plastic bowl with newspaper strips, one layer at a time, brushing the diluted glue over each layer. Press the glued newspaper against the sides of the bowl.

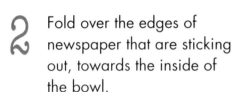

2 Fold over the edges of newspaper that are sticking out, towards the inside of the bowl.

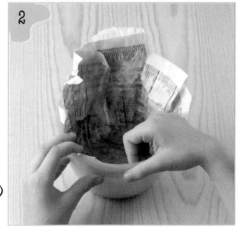

Toolbox

You will need:
- white glue
- orange, blue and white paints
- plastic bowl
- paintbrushes
- instant papier-mâché
- plaster of paris
- newspaper

3 When the paper bowl is dry, take it out of the plastic bowl. Use instant papier-mâché to make a thick rim around the edge of the bowl.

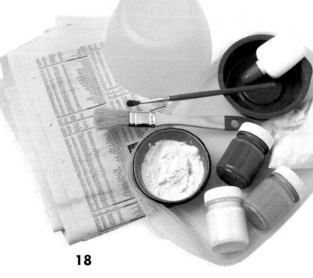

4 Brush plaster paste (see page 5) over the whole bowl. After the paste dries, paint the bowl orange with a blue-and-white striped rim.

5 With the tip of your finger paint blue and white spots all the way around the outside of the bowl.

Use this decorated bowl to store
coloured pencils, coins,
or any other small items.
It should never be used for food or drinks.

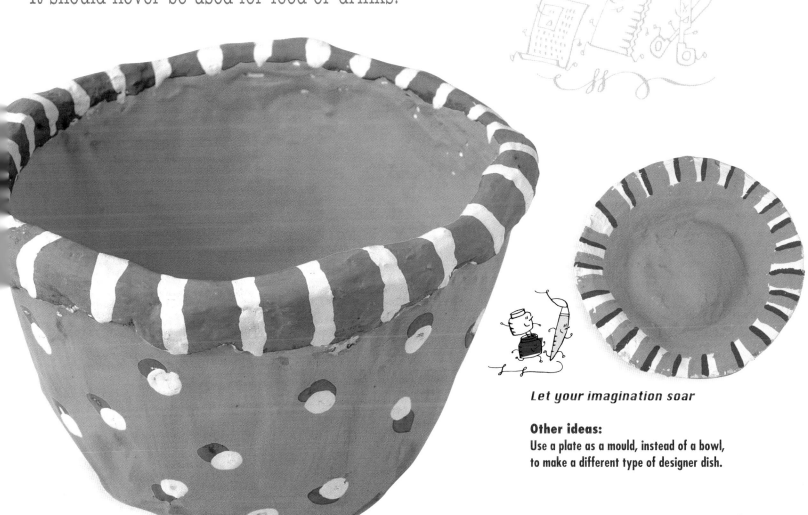

Let your imagination soar

Other ideas:
Use a plate as a mould, instead of a bowl, to make a different type of designer dish.

Space Rocket

With a little imagination, even a papier-mâché rocket can take you into space. Follow these easy steps and you'll be on your way.

Toolbox

You will need:
- white glue
- paper
- newspaper
- 2 cardboard toilet tissue tubes
- black, white, red and orange paints
- paintbrushes
- cocktail stick
- plaster of paris
- scissors

1 Dilute white glue with water, then tear paper into strips. Use glue-soaked paper strips to attach a ball of newspaper to one end of a toilet tissue tube.

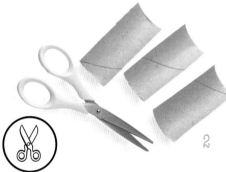

2 Cut another toilet tissue tube into three equal pieces.

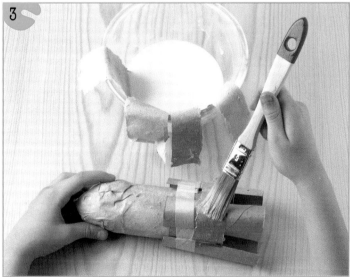

3 Using more glue-soaked strips of paper, attach the three pieces of cardboard tube around the open end of the rocket to make booster engines.

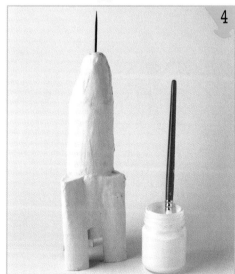

4 When the rocket and boosters are dry, paint a cocktail stick black and stick it into the tip of the rocket. Cover the whole rocket with plaster paste (see page 5) and paint it white.

5 Decorate the rocket with red squares around the body and paint the tip of the rocket black. Paint the tops of the booster engines red and paint the bottoms orange, making the orange paint look like flames.

10, 9, 8, 7, 6,
5, 4, 3, 2, 1...
Blast off!

Let your imagination soar

Other ideas:
Use modelling clay or instant paper-mâché to make the booster engines.

Box Turtle

Making this friendly turtle is fun and fast. Its shell is a cardboard egg box.

Toolbox

You will need:
- powdered glue
- scissors
- paper
- paintbrushes
- cardboard egg box
- newspaper
- masking tape
- green, orange, yellow, white and black paints

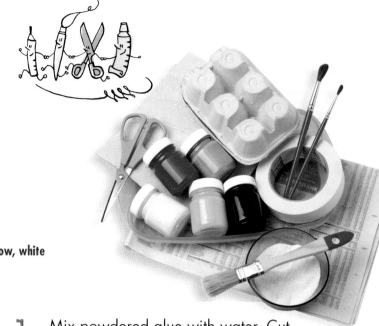

1. Mix powdered glue with water. Cut out four feet and a triangle-shaped tail from a piece of paper. Glue the paper shapes to the top of an open cardboard egg box so that two feet are sticking out on each long side of the box. The tail should stick out of one end.

2. Crumple newspaper and wrap it with masking tape to shape the turtle's head and neck.

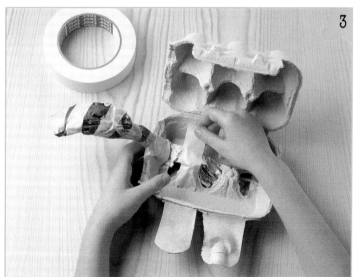

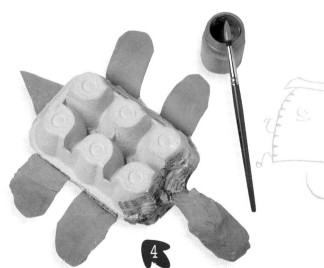

3. Attach the neck to the other end of the egg box from the tail. Cover the head and neck with glue-soaked strips of newspaper and glue the egg box closed with more glued strips of newspaper.

4. When all of the newspaper is dry, paint the head, feet and tail of the turtle green.

5 Paint the shell of the turtle orange with green and yellow details. Paint an eye on each side of the head and paint yellow claws on each foot. An orange mouth, a black nose and yellow stripes across the tail will finish your turtle off.

Your colourful turtle may be too slow to win a race, but it's sure to win smiles.

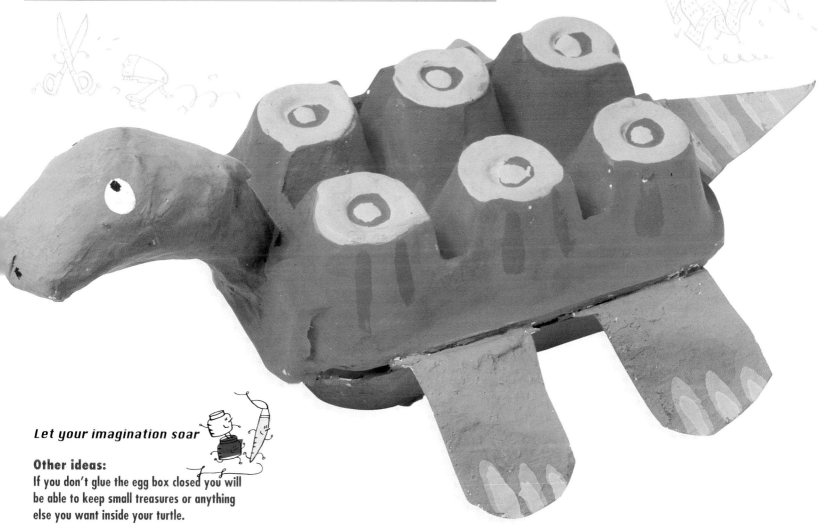

Let your imagination soar

Other ideas:
If you don't glue the egg box closed you will be able to keep small treasures or anything else you want inside your turtle.

Roly-poly Person

Imagine a roly-poly doll that never falls down. Now make one!

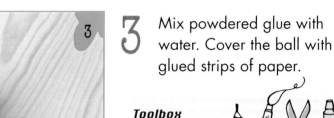

1 Fill half of a plastic ball with modelling clay, pressing the clay against the inside of the ball with your fingers.

2 Place the other half of the plastic ball on top of the clay-filled half. Stick masking tape around the ball to hold the halves together

3 Mix powdered glue with water. Cover the ball with glued strips of paper.

Toolbox

You will need:
- scissors
- modelling clay
- plastic ball that separates into halves
- masking tape
- powdered glue
- paper
- pink, blue, white, green, orange and red paints
- cardboard egg box
- paintbrushes

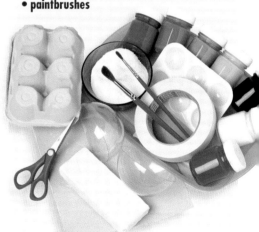

4 When the glued paper is dry paint the top half of the ball pink and the bottom, clay-filled half blue.

24

6 To make a hat, cut one cup out of a cardboard egg box. Paint the outside of the cup blue. When the paint is dry decorate it with white and green spots. Glue the hat to the top of your roly-poly person.

5 Paint hair and a face on the pink top of the ball and paint stripes or other decoration on the blue bottom.

Push the roly-poly person forwards and backwards and all around. It will tip over but never fall down!

Let your imagination soar

Other ideas:
If you don't have a plastic ball use modelling clay to shape the bottom of the doll and make the top out of crumpled newspaper. Then cover the whole figure with glued paper.

Funny Face

You'll have to use your head to make this clever clown mask, but don't use it to shape the mask's face! Use a balloon instead.

Funny Face Funny Face Funny Face

Toolbox

You will need:
• white glue
• balloon
• newspaper
• paintbrushes
• scissors
• instant papier-mâché
• craft knife
• bradawl
• plaster of paris
• different coloured paints
• glue stick
• green paper garland
• black elastic

1 Dilute white glue with water. Blow up a balloon and knot the end. Cover one side of the balloon with damp strips of newspaper, brushing each strip with diluted white glue.

2 When the newspaper is dry, pop the balloon. Cut off the uneven ends of the newspaper to shape the edge of the mask.

4 Ask an adult to cut eye-holes in the mask with a craft knife and to make small breathing holes below the nose with a bradawl. Also use the bradawl to make a hole near the edge on each side of the mask, just below the eyes.

3 To make a nose for the mask, roll instant papier-mâché into a ball and press it onto the centre of the mask.

5 Cover the whole mask with plaster paste (se page 5). When the mask is dry paint it any way you like.

6 To make the clown's hair use a glue stick to attach a coiled strip of green garland to each side of the mask.

7 Thread black elastic through the two holes in the edge of the mask. Knot both ends to hold it in place.

When you want to make people laugh put on your funny face. Don't be surprised if no one recognises you!

Let your imagination soar

Other ideas:
Use instant papier-mâché to shape animal ears and a nose to make an animal mask. Attach the ears to the top of the mask instead of hair.

Mâchémobile

Trying to work out how you made this creative car will drive your friends crazy! The secret is cardboard tubes and papier-mâché.

1 Mix powdered glue with water. Glue three cardboard tubes together in a row and two more on top of them (as shown). Hold the tubes in place with pegs until the glue dries.

2 Soak torn strips of newspaper with the diluted glue. Wrap the strips around the cardboard tubes until the tubes are covered with newspaper.

Toolbox

You will need:
- powdered glue
- green, white, black and yellow paints
- 5 cardboard toilet tissue tubes
- clothes pegs
- plaster of paris
- paintbrushes
- newspaper

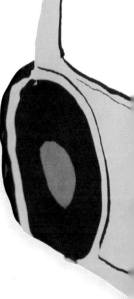

3 When the newspaper is dry, cover the whole car with plaster paste (see page 5) and paint it green.

4 Paint the windows of the car and the front and back registration plates white.

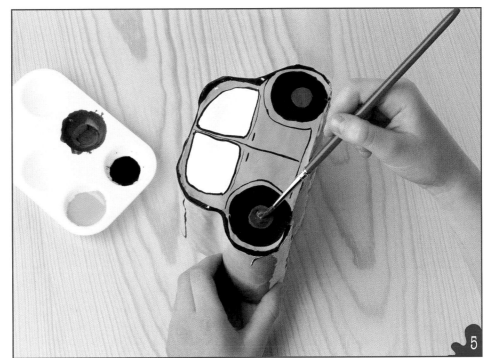

5 Paint wheels and other details on the car black and paint yellow lights on both the front and back ends.

This clever car is a great decoration, but it is also sturdy enough for playtime.

123456

Let your imagination soar

Other ideas:
Use more cardboard tubes or use paper towel roll tubes to make larger vehicles, such as tractors or trucks.

Easter Bonnet

A yellow flower adds a splash of colour to this pretty purple hat. Wear it proudly at a party or for any other special occasion.

Toolbox

You will need:
- scissors
- purple paper
- bowl
- powdered glue
- newspaper
- masking tape
- paintbrushes
- green and white paints
- yellow cardboard
- white glue

1 Cut strips of purple paper so they are a little longer than the diameter (width) of the bowl you will be using.

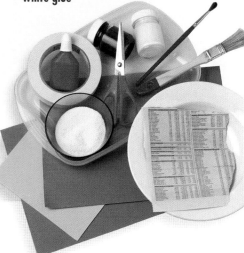

2 Mix powdered glue with water. Cover the bowl with a layer of purple strips without using glue. Then add one or two more layers of strips that have been brushed with glue.

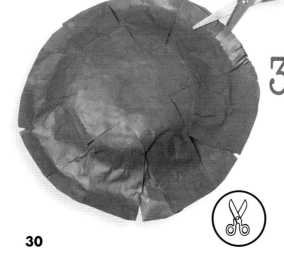

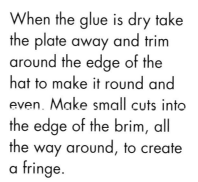

3 When the glue is dry take the plate away and trim around the edge of the hat to make it round and even. Make small cuts into the edge of the brim, all the way around, to create a fringe.

4 To make the stem for the flower decoration roll newspaper into a thin strand that is long enough to fit around the crown of the hat. Wrap masking tape around the newspaper and paint the stem green.

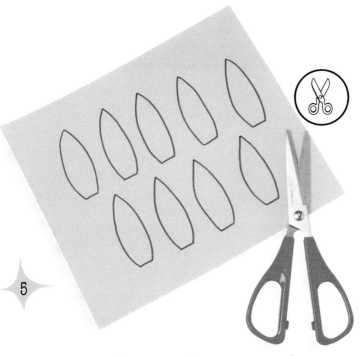

5 Draw nine flower petals on a piece of yellow cardboard and cut them out. Use white glue to stick the petals to the end of the green stem.

6 Push a small ball of newspaper into the centre of the petals and paint it white. Use white glue to stick the flower stem to the top of the hat.

Just wait and see how elegant you look in this fancy hat!

Let your imagination soar

Other ideas:
Instead of adding a flower, glue a long piece of yellow ribbon around the top of the hat and let the ends of the ribbon hang from the back.

Papier-mâché

Working with papier-mâché teaches children a new technique for modelling and creating using very simple materials: glue, water and paper. This technique makes it possible to recycle all sorts of paper (newspaper, used writing paper, pieces of wrapping paper, etc.) for a creative purpose.

Following are some suggestions for making each project, as well as a guide to the most appropriate age level of each one. It is important to point out that the suggested age is based on the degree of difficulty of the process, but the projects can be easily adapted to varying age levels.

p.6 **Friendly Ghost.** To simplify the project, it can be done with coloured paper and two pieces of sticky tape on top for the eyes.
Ages 5 and up

p.8 **Bright Bird.** The bird's feet can also be made with newspaper rolled up and held in place with sticky tape. In this way the number of materials needed is reduced, but this means that the bird's legs are less mobile.
Ages 6 and up

p.10 **Hot-air Balloon.** Older children can make the balloon's basket with wicker to learn to use other materials and techniques.
Ages 7 and up

p.12 **Handsome Hanger.** The project can be finished with paint, but it is essential to varnish it so that once dry, the hanger can be used to hang clothes on.
Ages 6 and up

p.14 **Little Red Devil.** The puppet's costume can be simplified if it is done with stapled or glued crepe paper.
Ages 7 and up

p.18 **Designer Bowl.** Younger children can do the edge with modelling clay or leave it smooth to make the project much simpler.
Ages 5 and up

p.20 **Space Rocket.** If the base is covered and a slot is cut in the upper part of the tube, the rocket can be used as a money box.
Ages 6 and up

p.22 **Box Turtle.** To simplify the project the head of the turtle can be made flat, like the legs.
Ages 5 and up

p.24 **Roly-poly Person.** If it does not stand upright the figure can be balanced by adding more papier-mâché where necessary to act as a counterweight and give it stability.
Ages 6 and up

p.26 **Funny Face.** This is easier to do if the balloon is placed in a holder of some kind, such as a bowl, while it is being covered with the paper.
Ages 7 and up

p.28 **Mâchémobile.** The base of the car can also be made using two boxes of different sizes. Place the larger one under the smaller and then follow the rest of the instructions in the same way.
Ages 6 and up

p.30 **Easter Bonnet.** It is easier to make the flower if appropriately coloured tissue paper is used to make the stem and petals.
Ages 5 and up